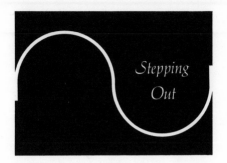

Stepping Out

Carolyn Stoloff — Stepping Out

1971 SANTA BARBARA UNICORN PRESS

The author wishes to thank the editors of the following magazines, in which many of these poems first appeared, for permission to reprint: *Antioch Review: Carleton Miscellany; Chelsea; Choice; Columbia Forum; Gallery Series II; Graffiti; Hearse; Kayak; The Nation; New York Times; Northwest Review; Outsider; Poetry Northwest; Poetry Review; Unicorn Journal; University Review* and *Yale Literary Magazine.*

ACKNOWLEDGEMENTS
"The Austere Place" first appeared in the *Yale Literary Magazine,* © 1962; "Black Shoes" first appeared in *Gallery Series II,* © 1968 Artcrest Products; "Linger" first appeared in *Northwest Review,* © 1961; "Triptych" first appeared as a separate Unicorn Press chapbook, © 1970.

Unicorn Press books are published by the Unicorn Foundation for the Advancement of Modern Poetry, Inc., P.O. Box 1469, Santa Barbara, California 93102.

The author wishes to express her gratitude to the MacDowell Colony where a number of these poems were written. Thanks, too, to Sonya Dorman for her invaluable comments and encouragement over years.

Library of Congress Catalogue Card Number 70-168608
International Standard Book Number 0-87775-026-2

FOR MY MOTHER AND FATHER

TABLE OF CONTENTS

I

II

III

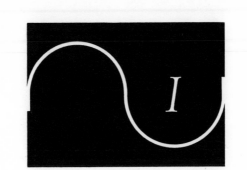

INTERSECTION

Hey you, switch your eyes on!
Signals click, columns
march synchronized into the distance.
     With luck

and a little skill I'll cross
the intersection. A hand
works at a windshield where a blind
     spot sticks.

The shuttle from spine to foot
locks. Puppets gawk
after an empty truck. A cop
     barks;

the pouch unzips, spilling
surgical tools. Knees,
hems, trouser cuffs. They buzz
     and nudge.

What do they mean — those quick
gestures and judging fingers?
I am hurt — I feel certain.
     Quit

pushing, he says, stretching
to look. It is I who lie open
to traffic. The whole sky
     is green.

BLACK SHOES

Two big black shoes
two feet apart
two black male shoes
with holes where the laces
were taken out
both big black heavy shoes
smooth where the feet were
black leather hard
old shiny shoes too
far apart on the platform

Who kicked them off in the subway
who shook them off
took the laces too
who pulled the laces out carefully
big black shoes full of soul smell
where did your man fly off to
tattered grey guy with a toothpick
out through a hole
in the city's arse
up to the silver sky
with a fat cigar

BIRDS IN REVIEW

Minds wracked with wind,
swift as some words, they wheel
pooled over my Sunday world
gifted with stiff-fingered wings.

They brake, sundazed, and flurry
as one, two, far-off-floating few
are drawn from the unzoned fields
to squadron with the fluttering flock.

Oval shadows shinny a fence, riddle
the rubble, take to the reeling
height. I watch them rise
to dots; slide to a grim return.

In a severe attack of will they spill
from blue to strafe my silent
tenement, zoom, solid
into my crossed panes and scram.

CHRISTMAS DAY

Christ ma   stay
the world is a lonely play
no horse
no place to lie
no where warm

Cold black ash
leafs from the sky
settles on a rim   on a lip
stars rattle in a dry
gourd   tap tap

Cash in a brown bag
buys a bloody bone
buys a withered wreath
buys a roof
a soupspoon

Stay ma   of the night
I was born   fourteen
thousand nine hundred
and eighty five days
ago   I don't remember
a thing

A CAT SCREAMS
Croton-on-Hudson

a cat screams
outside   blackness drips
a moth lays eggs
in my palm

soon I will be all holes
soon wind
will move through me
through the whole house:

a black cat pouring
across the white chenille
bedspread
clogging chimneys

threading wood's
secret channels   a child
screams   alone
in a universe all holes

NOTHING LIKE A RAZOR

and the movement
          of a wrist to wipe
a life. Foam slips
          off, barbarian
scum. Blood
          and a swarm of nightingales
at the faucet sing. Cling
          to the sink, brink
of a white count —
          down; maybe Trajan, closed
in a room with its stink
          and steam, blew
his nose too, coughed
          up the phlegm then
with silk
          cheek, loomed
into view
          over them.

FALSE REPORT

N.Y. *Times Sept. 27, 1962*

They brought up the artillery   a bunch of guys
in stiff uniforms with belts
of shining rockets surrounded
the royal pad   and they went AKAKAKAK
            and freezers quit purring and sleek
            cadillacs were trapped in their stalls
                   but HE
stood regal and full of nails
Mohammed   sonofan Imam   Ahmad of Yemen
a week on the throne and they bop bop bop shotimup
and he stood cheeky   as twelve
rings slipped
from his fingers
as sweet blood spread on his white burnoose
the holes spread and sky
poured in the palace caved in the whole
sheBANG crushed his full lips of women
and a blue vein spilled from his marble head   he had
a long thin
nose in the photos and a neat
beard and a ring
around each velvet eye that watched
the crows go white
around him   but he was human
he even went to the Soviet Union to get help
HELP youguys HELP he said
me to ACTivate CULTivate and EEE-
lectify my country   but it was TOO
late time's UP
for thoseguys   GEEEs they must have been REAL
MAD to have made suchamess

                          THINK man
he might have come to the States with a bushel
of pens to hand out with IMAM
MOHAMMED OF YEMEN engraved
IN GOLD   he was not
old and he was an aRISto CAT
and it makes me sad to see
allofem go   especially one
with a TAG like that.

18

SPRING 1968

Listen to the apple core
every apple has one
four glass tulips two cigars
war and revolution

Black men swallow candied dice
bone forgets its marrow
bankers count out grains of rice
but oh — the grave is narrow

Fighting through the flesh of sleep
seeds bang in their pockets
kiss the dead and do not weep
poverty breeds rockets

Christ walks silent in the street
Harlem children have no feet
judges crouch in every town
on the way to Washington

SO I LIE

The truth doesn't need my cloth
so I needle life
into shape, a little less,
a barking dog. I intend to lie.
The truth, whining,
takes the wrong road, while I
arrange numbers as though the direction
were not always down. But what
about a dog's bark
could remedy the ache
for leapt years, for flesh
in the teeth, its naked taste.
One can only squeeze the sponge
hoping it soaked up something just,
unheard, one humble lie.

STEPPING OUT

If I could collect jewels
from broken strings rolling
on the floor of feeling
to sort into bowls labelled
by cut clearness and color

I'd step out nightly
clapping like a gypsy,

with foreign tongues spangling
my wrists, a hail of crystal
eyes at my neck — loop
upon loop, and in my hinged ring
the garnet of your heart.

OPPOSITES

What could we do, he and I:
the Norseman who didn't discover America,
and I, candy-striped from a Turkish Bazaar?
What would we do together?
I, a lithe coconut palm nodding by an oasis,
he, a huntsman trudging
up to his waist in snow.
How could he catch me,
his line baited with minnows
to tempt a dolphin from the dense sea?
What call could he utter
through those linear lips
that would move my lusty hull
to rock him safely on night waters?
How could the same house hold us?
me with my frozen fingers,
him with his mango desire.

LINGER

and loan me
your idle
lily-white
tissue.
Lonely, I
am whiling
away my time-
less change-
ability. Teach
me honey
that melo-
dious incantation
full blown
from the lips of your
felicity. Lean
on my shoulder
lightly
till our limbs
lie limp
in the morning.
Dunce
in the hammock
of my longing
I'll learn
to my lung
capacity.

TODAY

hooks into the loop; the sun —
a lemon wafer on waxed
paper. God walks
the wall, warning me.
His shadow clears the glare
on picture glass.

                  Trucks
shatter the street, voices,
Japanese and shrill, sooty feet
stand on my sill, but no freight
of flesh moves through the harsh
element to this pier.
                     Will another death

                   bait me?
The bandage tightening on my art
I'll feign contentment, soothe
my hair, sip cool
drinks in summer, forget
                   I am not

remembered by you, dog-deep
in living, that I must let you lie.

THE TURNING

Felled, she lies half
buried in the snow.
He is a nomad; what
shall he make of her?

A tent pole he secures
in a high wind
as the canvas billows?

The canoe he carries on his back
to shoot the falls?
The paddle that he lost
the drift of? Or a gate post.

As he comes down the street
with the blind staggers,
he grabs for it
with one hand

and clutches his hat
with the other. *I'm tired,*
he says, and sinks
to its base for a minute.

A rib of the crib he holds
when he can't sleep,
when he is the rough,
loved up, old

teddy bear she can't
keep? Still the bole
turns.   Chips
fly out of reach.

She is a pencil;
the page is white.
Winter is a hand
too stiff to write.

LOVE ME OR NOT

I came, full of Chopin
knotted with flowers,
to this room where an odor of ashes
clings to wood and leather.
Love me or not, tonight's
a black
daisy, opening.

We have closed our books.
Our heads rest
against rough upholstery.
Not a thread of wind
no thud of pine cone to bruise
the naked darkness.
I may lose my mouth, or slip,
a bee, into the moon
if you lean over me.

But the smoke of your breath
hangs between. Birds
roost still
as beads on a crib as the huge
ant with a bright grain
of sand in his mandibles
crosses the night.
These lips will keep.

As you walk me home chatting
population, juvenile crime,
taking pains
to post your property,
to hold no gun, I'll open
my yellow umbrella
against the black petals.

When the sun jells and earth
rolls from my chest
may I whisper: *We spoke
one tongue in the towering night*
though scattered, babbling
food for war
though I find in my fist
a crushed newspaper.

WE WILL WALK BY THE TRAIL

We will walk by the trail, you to your home,
I to the place where the stone
wall breaks. You will remark on passages
where sun whitens the bare branches of a pine.
Delicate as the locust in our yard, you'll say,
in winter when it's topped by snow.
Icing on a chocolate cake, I'll toss back,
African with war paint! to top your simile
though I don't see it that way.
It's your memory. You were alone.
Having kissed your family, you closed the door.
Caught in the cool morning between house
and car, the tree struck
your fancy with sharp fragility.
Locusts in leaf are lovely, I'll say,
reaching for contact in the abstract,
They're better bare, you'll reply.
Yes, there's a certain chill in the air.
You're involved with words and winter; I'd wrap
green summer round my skin, disguise bone
facts, rings in the trunk, twisted roots,
under another truth as you poke thick ferns
with your stick to expose any lively thing
before it strikes, or begins to sing.

IF HE BUCKS

I was the only guest so there was breakfast, lunch,
dinner between us, otherwise hot sun at noon, thorns,
abandoned shafts, the strong stuff, unburned
below. We did not speak of it. You sipped
Seven Up and bragged of the observatory, a dot
on a distant peak.

The cords of your neck's back were so naked I turned
from them shamed as by a starved dog. Your lips
were dry with gossip of Cordonas y Calientes.
With the voice of a mailman stripped of his sex
you webbed the valley with passionate relationships.
You said: *If he bucks, free your feet from the stirrups.*

I should have told you not to yank the reins.
You wore sharp iron at your heels. For flight?
At night we played gin.
I wondered — under the engraved silver buckle
that held the jeans on your thin hips, were there stars
on your belly? You won, continually.

If he bucks, free your feet from the stirrups,
was your advice. We almost touched once
or twice as I erased God with me as his prophet,
but you were right, it was late. If there were stars
there were stripes, thick as bars,
so I turned in; freed my feet from the boots.

II

MONDAY, NOVEMBER 25, 1963

Drugged, we sit on air beyond rooms of belonging.
Roosts, nests of us, freeze.
Torn stripes hang, windless, from clotheslines.
Behind shutters, on kitchen chairs,
we crackle wrappers between numb fingers.
Almost all the leaves have fallen.

Almost all the leaves had fallen on the lawns
when I lost my self in the vault of the event.
Even he was lost in the cathedral;
he forgot breakfast, forgot the telephone,
he forgot his stiff spine all over again.
The cathedral was larger than his absence.

All of us left the beds of our dying that day;
all felt blood on our tongues at the railing.
It was the body of the land he became,
its dust, the host we swallowed.
Cannon continued to boom.
Candles fell into formation.

I have dressed my lips in black.
The soldiers of my fingers march
in black uniforms with the cortege
behind the packed box, under the river of the sky.
Pockets empty, on kitchen chairs,
we listen to the drums.

IN THE NAME OF HEAVEN

Why must the angel warn
me with a cook's mouth to retreat
by the narrow street
from which I came, hungry,
to this land of wheat and leisure?

Who hid the moon with swarms
of locusts, thick as a hand, in the name
of heaven, when I would leap the craters
of the night, desert my weight, dare
anything for pleasure?

After a winter sleep —
the serpent's truth: the wise
tongue I swallowed that whispered
in my mother's ear, *Allow*
nakedness its pleasure,

as the seed splits and the river
floods the furrow; release
in earth's excess, the flesh
made Father.

When the time comes, I'll bear
my cross of paper up
the hill to the last
ruthless act, but now
let's lie together.

THROUGH THE ARCH

Blue-eyed boys strut through the arch;
pre-triumphant, cheeky, they march
to break blood, to steel victory.
They've volunteered for this thrust
at the sire, this first flesh-offering
to fire as eyes peel them in strong sun.
Fife and drum declare them
not adolescent boys prepared with words
for afternoon's disasters,
but knights, bright as brass.
No harm will come.   Let them pass!
Weeds, delicate and green, root
between stones; when the real
war begins, loose for the throwing,
they will rain upon old men, weak
in their wisdom, whom these young become.

COME NEAR

Come near, the beat of boots
echoes, you cannot hear
me through this war.   A pale
moon rises and the gully steams;

a cavalry has passed between us.
Winter's greedy. Stars burn,
fall, are snuffed.   Around smoking
twigs tough men crouch, arms

outstretched to bless the dust.
As shadows join hill to hill
the grudge against unarmed
flesh you carry like a pack

may drop. Come near and hear
blades bend, lilies open.
Unstrap your helmet
before the grass is broken.

WIND AND THE EARTH

Wind sighs with the breath of obsessed
women, sighs around thick bodies of men
who will be swayed but not uprooted,
who move with the earth, in their own ground.
Wind sighs for obsessed women who would possess
them, the men who will not be possessed.
Wind probes cracks in bark.
Trees loosen their leaves for wind
but will not be moved.   Earth travels,
trees with it. The heavy
fertile earth without eyes revolves
feeding the trees through roots it holds,
lets them branch, stretch, be swayed,
sleeps in the flesh of women who are not greedy,
who simply let seeds grow.

GARDEN OF DOLLS

I have walked through a door of air into the blue-
winged wind on the edge of wet; lying against glass
I awaited myself, expecting dahlias
to bloom in this garden of dolls.

Buttocks, scapulas, knees: crooked doors into a house
of toys whose tin surfaces call for keys
the wrack has hidden with my father's eye.
Here I await women whose mansions are windowless.

A GRADUAL ACCRETION
for Sonya Dorman

A crystal on a core grows
              in solution. To observe
every line, thrust, rainbow
              is impossible, yet
oversight invites sleep's refusal.
              Not to will
but finger in the dark a leaf
              edge, the curved
continuous contour of a shell
              the detail in bark
its tunnelling beetles
              is to trust nerve
but gamble on losing muscle
              in the fall
through canyons of light.

On a column of pine a squirrel
              trails a spiral.
As his paw lowers
              my still fingers
with the careful removal
              of what I offer
I revolve on my axis to divine
              in solution, a budge, yes
a quivering nuzzle.

POSTHURRICANE

Fire Island Pines, April 1962

I would not
go past insane
umbrella spines to the beach
where tangerines flame
in the wrack and a cotton
dress swings in a closet's
black mouth.

If gulls screech
and grow fat, if scavengers
collect clocks, knockers,
coffee pots, pitched
to the hide and seek,
let them, I would not.

But I did
come down to doors,
beams, and split crates:
a maze for the curious
to knock about in, unhinged
by the wind.

Too squeamish to pick
at smashed scenes: glass
crumbs on the sea's
table, freezers, broilers,
fixtures of dreams etched
with sweat, I did not.

But I did
gape, got a charge
at a bargain rate.
The old bull, back
from pasture, stuck his wet
snout in these juvenile
structures, his kick on the bare
boardwalks, and there's

a certain poetic justice
about Weathertite to the waist
in spume, in wild-become-warehouse
freed of use again.
There had been too many frame
dwellings, not mine,
too close.

Hearing my reflection,
the sea scrambles to my feet.
My shoes are wet
before I can run
from my philosophical position.

LEGACY

Penitent for bottles, chairs, china
smashed, you married her,
prepared to tackle twists,
to fold your brokenness in her gold
flesh. Patiently you probed
her fear of heights, cracks, crowds,
aloneness in the night. Reins slack,
you horsed around, ploughed
her loose ground until the blade
caught, then, exhausted, left
still loving. She bent you back,
repaid her debt in the cash
of torment, that at this hour
in any room you smell the gas,
and feel her beyond the door
revive her calculated legacy.
You watch a fly buzz
out of reach and speak your speech:
I am a needful boy, greedy
for life; she was the birth,
the mandible of pain, the earth
I crave but won't be buried in. And yet
you writhe between the lethal sheets.

BEYOND THE PARALLEL LINES

sharpened by point of view, steep cliffs
he crawled through; larks, trapped
in lucent amber as they passed; beds
of streams deepened by smiles — at what?
The curse of distant vision has come true
and he forgets. Deep in the mirror
swift tracks meet in mystical rapport.
His sons ski on his slope, watch sport
become war within the pattern
of the court. Tense for the stroke
his will stops short. The blade
debates; stubble sprouts with insidious
force. The train will leave
at 7:49 a.m.; it will not wait
for him. He lifts
the razor; tracks
diverge beyond their vanishing.

FOR THE SUICIDE'S DAUGHTER

In the narrow
> closet under the stairs, its curved
> claws retracted in ferocious fur, the bear
> slept long after they found her curled
> on the tiled floor, as in the parlor

grave
> and correct relatives revolved
> among the stuffed chairs murmuring:
> *Dreadful accident. Shocking thing*
> *to happen. Poor child;* but you,

the child
> who had laughed in the circus of her skirts,
> caught the smell of the broom closet
> in the empty glass she left,
> though they rinsed it well, and

sat
> choked but defiant. *Cat*
> *got your tongue?* You were sure. *Say PLEASE*
> *and it's yours.* You knew, but you couldn't
> say it so you screwed up your face,

tasting
> the clean bite of silence. *Watch out!*
> warned the aunts and cousins, *it will freeze*
> *that way.* They wondered if the tight cords
> would bend, as they stood between you and

the ritual of naming.
> At bedtime, sweat formed
> on your child's palm, still creased
> with wisdom from the wet, as you crept
> up the steps, cautious.

One night,

      deep in your dilations, the winter tongue awoke.
      Bear! you called. *Bear, BARE,* at the door.
      Lye. Lye, LIARS, you screamed
      as the glass broke.

Older

      you stamped as you climbed to the man
      who came to board up the closet, to strum
      as you clapped in your tall
      mother's shadow, rapped

in the skin

      of her heat and color, as you
      tapped with your heels: *Look! there is no*
      hell or punishment, no hollow
      place under this land.

You spoke,

      bare in the night room, with intense
      gestures: *No furs for me,*
      or ribbons either. Instead, retrievers,
      named, responsive, and through the dark

a girl

      feels her way freely to find her
      doors to open. In the kennel
      dogs bark. Between their paws rest
      the bones of cold dancers.

HER YELLOW ROSES

We flock to the pier and wave as she stands
at the railing her arms full of yellow roses,
a birthday of burning petals,
a dozen bright days to smile in.

If the wound of her blooming undressed doubt,
if her thorns braved fingering thieves
and suitors, petals wing from unbroken heads,
wicks of unlit wishes curl in satin coves
flooded with blue, with tides of Mediterranean
sleep that rise in havens of shadow.

If she forgets her roots as she fades
and we shiver home, still alive, she will slip
into water salted with Spain, shyly extend
a neck, wrinkled and thin, as she floats on the deep,
chaste, in her brown days.

BELLE

A glass bellied underwater wish blossomed
and forgot to sting. She's twins
doing things together. Watch!
double shell lids open
                          and close, breathing.

In summer weather she wears plastically daring
wingback earrings reclining in a deck
chair bundled to the neck
in silk, stunned skin
                          reaching for sun.

Came an entertainer who returned yearly to kill
a few days. For him she was willing
at one time to provide
but he was a wide
                          open town;

he took her for a ride which she enjoyed
and ducked her. Without a toy
those sleepy eyes browse.
Through the marshmallows
                          of her cheeks

a little girl peeks, spaniel neighborly. She pulls
the cable stitch uncurtaining a full
mouth of teeth. She's
                          going south ———

AT THE WOODSTOCK CEMETERY

Lush cropped lawn
little markers leaning
trees very green
pruned, sure to blossom.
Underneath spongy stones —
old eyes
fallen cherries.
Buttons from suits and vests
sorted out, in treasure chests
cling to their identities
when bones become anonymous.

What did you lose little girl?
Your pappa? your child-doll?
your muse?
Stand at the rail if you please
but don't slip through
to the pretty park.
A spider with many arms
waits in his sun-warmed parlor.
Will you walk?
Will you fly?
Friends fall away
from rich crops of hair.
These stones name but one I know,
one I knew thirty years ago.

A WARM MOIST LICKING US

for Sonya Dorman

A warm moist licking us we crunch-squelched
the stuttering last year's litter half crisp
still letter-shaped browns among grey climbed lines
calling us through a drop or two coming to meet
us with sharp stickers you pointing a child-
scribbled vine charring it black with winter
against snow for me name-rapped your blond
panting seeing-nosed from maybe rolling in muck
exclaimed at beak-picked wounds in the tree
trunk that would not bear or be next year
its wood your woods updying
every last bulldozed even those massive haunts
overgrown bushes riddled summers with winged
instruments bringing their broods worms
bugs bringing them up even those old tough whiskers
torn from earth's face only the unrooted
marble plaques propped against trunks on the hill
making that place sacred would be unturned
as though collapsed calcium could curse or leaf
and live trees not   graceful barbarian this land
shorn raked flattened to private plots rowed
with civilized mausoleums will be mourned oh mourned
by us the partridge the rabbit the racoon the fox

POET IN TOWN

Eyes rising from under ponds
of classes, you, scholarly to the blunt
point of a pun, run
from those who love you, who would hold
you even by a long cord
like a dog in the dangerous country. Lonely
loose-jointed and afraid of nothing
but nobody, quietly frantic in your hotel
you call from the deep dictionary well
for a touch of warmth, a short stop
in somebody else's tomb. A seance
of lips, a clutch of fingers across
the tilting table of your sleep, and you drift
off dazed, an avatar wrapped
in unravelling momentary cloth.

THE WEAVER

for Alice Adams

Her hair a nest of silk threads
a child let slip, she curves
over the loom to follow the bobbin
but not until the last line
combs into place will she know
what she has. The pattern shifts
full of gold, cadmium red, tangerine,
uncertain whether to be sun
field of wheat, corn kernel
ready to burst with warm milk
a yellow mop, or one
ever opening bloom
of colossal chrysanthemum.

THE POTTER

for Dan Gehan

less form than line leans
over himself, listening. His hands
coil the length and breadth of women
with fused legs, hollow waiting bellies.
Mouths at the neck, they sound: wells
with no stones dropped in.
Lacking water they surround
him whose slim nose points
north, whose eyes look aside
to invisible fountains. With eloquent
stillness he draws land
untasted into a blind
country of battered shells.

CHRONICLE

for Jean

Lost in the shower of faucets
in clashing cymbals, dishes
it's March — I've lost my hands
cold crockery cuts
my ankles and the wheels split

The children tug my apron
wounds in their faces open
they squeeze me, screaming, with tears
in April a clatter, a hail
the roof of my mouth is frozen

They mount my thighs their ponies
to pummel the toys of my breasts
their toys, my breasts, their rabbits
to pick at my eyes' raisins
as their fevers rise in May

June — I vacuum around them
roots stamped in the soil
not to be reached with reason
thorns in my flesh, they bloom
their joints the hips of my roses

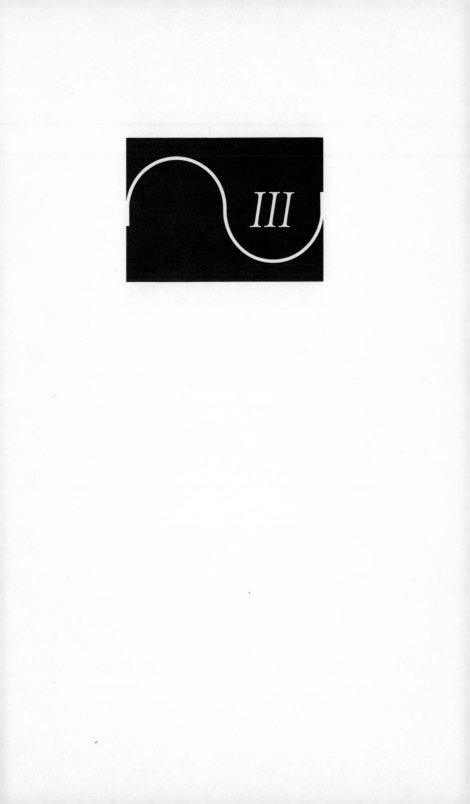

IS THIS THE PLACE?

Awakened from death in a strange city
by a bolt of sun, or a maid's key —
the closet door is ajar
in a hotel room that smells of hot paper.

Voices scribble the ear; a bell rings;
a squeal in the works of a clothesline;
engines rattle the knobs of a chest;
scooped out, we have no defense. From nests

of linens we rise, damp, stripped
of familiar hands. There's nothing to do
but ripple the broad calm of avenues
trailing a wing and a shadow
across the piazza at noon. If we dip

in narrow streets to pry for local graffiti
we see pigeon women at windows,
heavy breasts on sills of their arms,
mouths full of names: Giovanni,
Leonardo, Armando, plump as worms.

Our parade of loons floats by
unconcerned policemen; greedy eyes
widen to old geography. We pass
barriers of backs. Is this the place?

We feel a tug at the sleeve
and wheel, ready to dive.
A boy with something to sell!
We reach out — to touch a wall.

MORNING

When strings of diamonds cling to our coats
and haze rouges these bald facades,
when trucks bud with twitching heads
cooped for market, we wait for the light.

In castellated towns cogs lock
in fugue, cruel as watchworks in gyration,
jewels ride the toes of beaked tradesmen
as around huge corners I stalk
yesterday's steps through cubes of shadow.

Lamp posts tick, a window
burns, steel girders defy
and restrict space, but the curved eye
peers through the bars, and grows.

TOUR

She hungers for a scratch, to pull
space to surface, to surpass
by clutching at a rasp
of edge.

She wonders how it was when bones
of Stonehenge rose. Did thorns prick
where petticoat peonies droop?
The wild

is washed away; on level
lawn the daisy grows. Get her
among stones that now
mean

no more than bubbles in a tinted
pane, among plants rooted in turned
land to tangle with tough
ants.

She cannot salvage anything. Hills
roll in lumbering waves, what's
near rips past
as post card

parks advance and towers rear,
fade, leaving a hint of water-
color brush. Let's make
this trip

sensuous, more charged than retrospect
would dare, infuse her lungs with English
air, slip her a death
to touch.

SEA-AIR-ISLAND

Sea

flinging wrack, moss and mangled kelp
in a low hedge, you show, old wizard
where I shouldn't go. But who'll salvage
and edit your art from cool stones

on the shifting plate but me, tossed
in your junk-strewn passage up the ledge
moonstone myself, whelped in liquidity and land
polished by the grating of your breaking edge.

Air

no ninny-finned fish can know you bare
yowling on bluffs, in bayberry, only me
hunting a hidden moon with hands
that stumble on hanks of the island's pelt

risen to muff and mitten the gale
to cough fog, to match the sneezing sea.
In buffeting rush I place a sail
against my lips and blow.

Island

because you block my passage with your cliffs
holding the halved and hollow cockles
of my heart, I press my sharp shell to your flank
and soil my nails in your tough, bullish back.

TRIPTYCH

I

She was with grief
unstrung   foam split
                snuffed
                scattered
silk of dandelion fluff
sigh-borne   and tossed
down early morning haze
by this
this crucifer who turned away

Her eye reaps
from the bracing air
             a spray
and draws it   bachelor
across the dune
         white cheek
of holiday

No sacred heart
distills
her wounded vanity
        but Art
        hard crystal bottle
        holding it apart
deepens the color of the wine
and serves it   chilled

II

Slipped
by tide or intent
from shell
in haste
to recreate
to make ends meet
head down   his passage booked   into the steaming kettle
from the pot   claws pegged   he's held until all agitation
stops   Segmented
he who knows
the depths
cools
on the plate
The Patron
finds the meat
uncooked   not
to his taste
and leaves
him forked
and boiled
upon the table of the world   and eats the bait.

III

All   all is Calvary
and coward at the base
               his base
his bloody charity

Soft coffin in my ribs
child   railed and wailing
cribbed   roll on
and heal this garnet
bedded in my birth

(But no
not wheels
not surf of salt
can smooth   soothe
turn   this garbage
        of the sea's grief

her shale
   stuffed
   granite fault
       into a vacant brain
       wed page to image
   open up the vault)

BERMUDA NOTEBOOK

My notebook gone,
I covered my knees.

Lizards discovered my palm.
Ants rushed up

their highway on the white
column transporting

the invisible. Shadows slipped
from the sheet. I caught

my voice saying: *I have flown
through a gate*

*into a garden of yellow roses
into a noon of thorns.*

Earth passed its curved
blade across my eyes.

Without gifts, I expect
the black hand on the wall.
. . . .

I sent out tracers
left my number at the station.

Pen poised, on my porch
I waited. Clouds on a plate.

Plates of cloud in the cafeteria.
I speared one. It slid off.

Raindrops, no two alike,
scattered. Sparrows too.

What's a head, quipped the split
tail of a lobster. What's a notebook

with a blue cover to a ferrying man.
What's a bowl of blue with croutons

of cloud to a voice called John
who found it and chased me down.

John Mattis, cab-driver, what's
my face to you?

ARRIVAL AT ST. GEORGE

A finger points to my line   then the long
corridor carpeted with sea grass
that muffles impatient heartbeats·   I open
a drawer in the white room to find
in its darkness   directions   warnings
yes yes I will button my collar
when the goliath hour draws
jostling lobsters from the deep

Drapes billow and snap   beyond them
palm fronds   boats bobbing
the smacking blue paper sea
I walk naked through a red rain
of megaphones announcing stillness
bump my nose on pink flats
in a square whose cannon points waterward
against invasions of plastic women

Flamingo clouds plume upward
with lyrical immense gestures
a brushtip scatters a passage of birds
so small they might have flown
from under my nail

On a wall's dragoning backbone
medusa heads loosen serpents
of night-blooming cereus   as I climb
dusk descends through benches in the harbor
lights in the sky reflect the island
I unpack my voice

SEGOVIA

1958

Dry in my fanless person, brushed
clean of Spain, the golden evening grows
sharp, vocal animations crush
me, cars clang along below.

I stand at the window, mild,
thirsty, without ears. Not a stiff black
back do I know that passes, or a child.
my own tongue chokes me without talk.

Gaily the girls gather, chaining
their arms, off to the paseo in a flock.
Dusk collides with the low sun, staining
roofs with stilted shadows of the aqueduct.

Oh slow me, mute and mental when the street
is active. Here to spend the summer spell
abroad, coming voiceless, for all the neat
reasons. But the air is sweet here and gentle.

TOLEDO

1958

Against the vivid yellow of the Burial
grafted on space, priests
ceremonially flat and pale, pace
pivot and blow behind the altar rail.

There, where the map is red, gifts
to the church inquisitive have just
begun to rust. A guide insists
on more ascensions than the Greek launched.
They flare up, weightless, from the dust.

The damascene the merchant sold me
at a price looked fine shining
in the showcase of his gallery.
Toledo glistens too on sunny mornings
from across the moat.

Through spills of worn streets
under the cap of roofs, we take the high
spots of a national museum in stride:
the house one painter lives in,
where one other died.

Behind a shop a pride of boys
tap metal threads into a heraldry
of fleur-de-lis and storks, dreams
up their sleeves, fiefs of a dry city.

No decoration cloaks
the hills of rock that grow no grain
where twelve thieves starve in a gypsy hut.
The pins and earrings were no bargain.
The steel scissors don't cut.

THE AUSTERE PLACE

1958

To gather the scores of eyeless men
(black bands on the sleeve of Spain),
would blunt the corners where they stand, apart.
To blast the altar's agitated plan

or hold a glass up to wounds that smart
would court infection from the cups
where, once, his eyes watched our wild
diseases of the heart, the coins we dropped.

To split the church of Vera Cruz and catch
the mass of messages that curl and burn
like dust, or topple the stork's nest, propped,
a beggar's hat, upon the tarnished

dome, would be to steal their loaf
leaving charred crusts on the salted stone.
As the hunger of noon rubs a chin of sand
we reach for the tongue's bread to moisten it with wind.

To tell the white ox, altered,
haltered on the hill: *No, don't advance,*
stay still, would be to stop
unknown faces of the clock, or hope

to see his horns rise
beyond the hill. To snatch at flies
that coat the bull's thick hide
as blue fills the ring, is to admit

night has the ear. There, lace-white,
a full moon rides above the turrets' height;
we have no lungs to answer with, or light.

IN LISBON

1968

Between cushions at the Ritz,
a thousand gardeners' hands —
But wait —
In Lisbon, even at noon,
a breeze blows the burn away.
Sometimes from the dark — the in-
temperate continent, rain,
bringing sulphur and mud, buzzes
against glazed tiles, infants' scrubbed
faces, unlocks
stone chips set in white and black
patterns in pavements.

In harbor bars at midnight
waiters lay down trays to sing
of hunger with closed eyes. Peach
petals, sliced from a dark pit,
drop to the plate, sardines sizzle
on the grill, but no dreamers
leave or return, only boats
with the familiar haul. Dawn
opens vast lounges. Through
clear glass patrons come to ease
themselves. Rough hands slip
into a sea of poppies.

BEHIND THE STARCHED LIGHT
Hydra, Greece 1968

Behind the starched light, in the pistachio tree,
the cicada's infernal motor starts to ring.

A man with a few small fish on a string
pauses in the harbor's bight to watch a lady

copy bright boats along the quay as a boy,
with two goats on a rope, pokes, then yanks them in.

Masterfully turning her compliant body
in his hands, a shopkeeper drones compliments

through pins; his wife listens and brews strong coffee
behind the curtain. The cicada stops,

the struggle for preservation goes on. No one
suffers from bends. Sponges thrive and creep up.

Cats punctuate steps that ascend to rocks
above plumbers' tools roasting on a terrace

above the crusader against concrete stuck
to his binoculars, still as a carapace

left by an insect on his loggia.
At the last house an old woman exposes

three gold teeth as she shakes her grandson proudly
at the American lady who climbed all that way

to arrive at her own view of things and faces
the sun's disappearance, hears an agonized

bray echo the mainland. Across her cheek
a child's hand passes, or cool breeze from the sea

so saturated with ultramarine it dyes
every living thing. Before her — deep Greek

Hydra night, the persistent cicadas.

I WILL NOT GO TO MIKONOS
Hydra, Greece 1968

How white can a white be
how houses bleached beyond
that white I see behind
my eyes now   can there
be fewer than no trees
or breath of wind stronger
than how I hear it howl
from the sea   up the steep
steps that curve into white
terraces   pages whipped
from my fingers told me
white moths left their eggs
in my lifeline long ago

This mind-wind tears a man
from his woman's breast   tilts
tall masts   bears babies
from the mainland as though
tomorrow were yesterday
women weave in white caves
white wakes stitch the sea
what blue! what emerald!
what royal purple!

Mikonos, reduced to bone
worn amulet against tentacles
that drew island ships down
down through ink   Mikonos
host   nurse to hordes of us
your houses draped in white
sheets   wait for their true
owners to come home

BEARING IT

Metsovon, Greece 1968

Bodies lift burdens
sacked   to shoulders   to backs
carry wool to spin
twigs to burn   grain
water in earthen jugs
baked hollows for bearing   men
lift blocks of bone
building shells for shelter
holes to lie down in
to be warmed by women   wormed
into by infants   men love
marry   carry stones
and wooden bones   curved
roof tiles   raise
place   secure
these with mortar
women bend at fountains
catching flow in hollows
rise with transparent water
weight on shoulders   in breasts
bellies   men leave
staffs in hand   tear
down   batter   break
scatter what holds
ravish what's held   make
over   fill women's
baskets and bowls with fish
loaves   men
leave   come home again

HOW CAN A CHILD HOPE
ALONG AVENUES

Athens 1968

How can a child hope along avenues
addressed to freedom when coarse generals
hold even the iron hulks of seafaring souls
in their hands   their trapped crews
like so many Lilliputians   how can a child
walk in his father's shadow
when strangers with shaggy chins plunge their arms
into wells of blue between white windy islands
between the dead rocks of actual stars

AS THOUGH I DIDN'T KNOW
Nerja, Spain 1968

Who enters this tower?
I arrived here alone
through an isthmus of olive trees
rooted in bleached earth
through harsh stones
mountains without dwellings

Along white streets eyes
tugged at my chest like sick dogs
yet I came on
as one with a destination
their angry voices
a creaking bed

Who cancels distance
lays eggs in my skull
as though I didn't know
the discovery made at home
among fragments of plates
a pinch of salt

MORNINGS AND EVENINGS

Ubeda, Spain 1968

I

I stand before the door with crossed
arms watching my children chase
their small shadows   or search the valley

The valley   veiled in dust   does not yield
me its olives   only tormented stumps

Let them bend under hats
men who sow   who reap   they have stripped
my bark up to the armpits, yes,

I carry full jugs from the fountain
daily I bring them water

II

My back to the hill I water dust
before my door   children I have spewed
stick at the world's edge

Divided earth continues to yield
and mountains appear in my dreams
as the teats of a huge sow

Behind me smoked shanks hang
from the ceiling   my blood runs salt
as I sweep night into the valley

Yet the fountain continues to flow
and the Civil Guard parades at eight
mornings and evenings   to be sure
my breasts have not fallen

THIS SPAIN

Ubeda, Spain 1968

Oh where have you gone my accustomed self
cows lead me through streets without windows
on each burro   sneezing in straw
I am sat on by men in creased clothes

Climbing the town dump with shorn
sheep to this pueblo   to hot olive oil
escaping walls   gypsies call
from mouths of maids folding sheets
fill immense jugs with saetas

The old rest on stone seats over the valley
its fists of olive trees   sit among roses
roses   bleached by sun   let their petals go
exposing the yellow fur of their pubes

Men hiss at virgins' breasts   the strong
juice of bulls outrages my esophagus
it will not go down smooth   this Spain
my head clangs at midday   a donkey
brays as if in frantic copulation

Yet   nearby   a canary trills passages
of such limpid joy   that angels
carnations in their hair   lean from balconies
shaking fresh sheets into the sun

THROUGH INFINITE POINTS

Ubeda, Spain 1968

Bells split the blue
children squint up at hawks
outstretched on the blue sheet
the eternal maid with crossed
apron strings bends to dust
digame, digame   she sings
opening wounds in dry hills
watering the valley with red rivers

The color of blood hangs
from balconies   iron lanterns
severe traps for light
cast dark spears down
walls into the dust
where old women sit
black alphabet
against white walls   near doors
from which dusk will come
and swallows   tracing loops
through infinite points

STEPPING OUT was type-set in 11 Palatino by Achilles Friedrich and printed and bound by Elmer Pickard. This first printing consists of 1,500 copies of which the first thirty have been numbered and signed by Carolyn Stoloff. Typography by ALAN BRILLIANT.